The Wild World of Animals

Dolphins

Fins, Flippers, and Flukes

by Adele D. Richardson

Consultant:
Daniel K. Odell, Ph.D.
Research Biologist
SeaWorld Florida

Bridgestone Books
an imprint of Capstone Press
Mankato, Minnesota

Bridgestone Books are published by Capstone Press
1710 Roe Crest Drive, North Mankato, Minnesota 56003
www.capstonepub.com

Library of Congress Cataloging-in-Publication Data
Richardson, Adele, 1966–
Dolphins: fins, flippers, and flukes/by Adele D. Richardson.
    p. cm.—(The wild world of animals)
    Includes bibliographical references and index.
    ISBN-13: 978-0-7368-0825-5 (hardcover) ISBN-10: 0-7368-0825-6 (hardcover)
    ISBN-13: 978-0-7368-8071-8 (softcover)   ISBN-10: 0-7368-8071-2 (softcover)
    1. Dolphins—Juvenile literature. [1. Dolphins.] I. Title. II. Series.
QL737.C432 R53 2001
599.53—dc21

                                                                00-010181

Summary: A simple introduction to dolphins describing their physical characteristics,
habitat, young, food, enemies, and relationship to people.

Editorial Credits
Sarah Lynn Schuette, editor; Karen Risch, product planning editor; Linda Clavel,
    designer and illustrator; Kimberly Danger and Heidi Schoof, photo researchers

Photo Credits
Doug Perrine/Innerspace Visions, cover; Todd Pusser/Innerspace Visions, 4, 14;
    Thomas Jefferson/Innerspace Visions, 20
Francois Gohier, 10
Gregory Ochocki, 8
Jeff Rotman, 12, 16
Mark Newman/Bruce Coleman Inc., 18
PhotoDisc, Inc., 1
Visuals Unlimited/David B. Fleetham, 6

Printed in the United States of America in Eau Claire, Wisconsin.
013014   007993R

Table of Contents

dusky dolphin

dorsal fin

flippers

flukes

Fins, Flippers, and Flukes

About 42 kinds of dolphins live in the world. Dolphins have rounded bodies to help them swim. Dolphins steer through the water with the flippers on their sides. Tail flukes help push dolphins forward. Most dolphins have a dorsal fin on their back for balance.

flippers

the armlike body parts
on the sides of a dolphin

spotted dolphin

blowhole

FUN FACTS

Some dolphins can hold their breath for more than 15 minutes. They then come to the surface of the water to breathe.

Dolphins Are Mammals

Dolphins are mammals. Mammals are warm-blooded and have a backbone. Dolphins breathe air through a blowhole on the top of their head. The blowhole closes when they are underwater. Dolphins have skin that feels smooth like rubber.

warm-blooded

having a body temperature that stays the same; a dolphin's temperature does not change with the weather.

Amazon river dolphins

FUN FACTS

The Amazon river dolphin is the largest freshwater dolphin in the world.

Seas, Oceans, and Rivers

Dolphins swim in water habitats. Saltwater dolphins live in seas and oceans around the world. Freshwater dolphins live in the rivers of Asia and South America. Many dolphins dive deep underwater. They also jump high above the water.

habitat
the place where an animal lives

southern right whale dolphins

Life in the Pod

Dolphins often live in groups called pods. Pods sometimes join together to form a herd. Male and female dolphins mate during spring and early summer. Female dolphins usually give birth to one calf.

mate
to join together to produce young

FUN FACTS

A bottlenose dolphin's brain is about the same size as a human brain.

Dolphin Calves

Dolphin calves see, hear, and swim very well from the time they are born. Calves swim close to their mother's side. Dolphin mothers take care of calves for more than one year.

common dolphins

Pod Protection

Scientists study dolphins to see how they live. Some scientists believe pods help protect calves or sick dolphins from enemies such as sharks. These dolphins swim in the middle of the pod. The strong, healthy dolphins swim on the outside to protect the pod.

protect
to guard or to keep
something safe from harm

bottlenose dolphin

What Do Dolphins Eat?

Dolphins eat fish, squid, and octopus. They have round teeth to grab food. But dolphins do not chew their food. They swallow food whole. Some dolphins break large fish into smaller pieces by hitting them on the water's surface.

squid

a sea animal with a soft body, ten tentacles, and no backbone

killer whale

FUN FACTS !

The largest dolphin
in the world is the
killer whale. Dolphins
and whales belong
to the same family.

Echoes Underwater

Dolphins use echolocation to hunt. They send out clicking sounds under the water. The clicks echo off objects in the water. Dolphins then learn the size, shape, speed, and location of objects such as fish.

echolocation
using sounds to find objects

indo-pacific humpback dolphin

Dolphins and People

People often visit oceans and zoos to watch dolphins jump and play. Scientists study dolphins to understand how they use echolocation. You can help dolphins stay safe and healthy by not littering.

Hands On: Keeping Water Clean

Dolphins live healthy lives in clean water. Some people litter and throw objects or chemicals into the water where dolphins live. This experiment shows how a small amount of a chemical can move through water and into the path of a dolphin.

What You Need

Plastic gallon (4-liter) jug
Blue food coloring
Water

What You Do

1. Fill the jug half full of water.
2. Put a few drops of blue food coloring in the water. Do not stir the water.
3. See how long it takes for all the water to turn blue.

The food coloring slowly moves through the water. This also is how chemicals move through oceans, seas, and rivers. You can help dolphins and other water animals by not littering.

Words to Know

calf (KAF)—a young dolphin

dorsal fin (DOR-suhl FIN)—the fin that sticks up from the middle of a dolphin's back

echolocation (ek-oh-loh-KAY-shuhn)—using sounds to locate objects; dolphins use echolocation to hunt.

flipper (FLIP-ur)—the armlike body parts on a dolphin's side; flippers help dolphins balance while swimming.

herd (HURD)—a large group of dolphins; many pods join together to form a herd.

mammal (MAM-uhl)—a warm-blooded animal with a backbone; dolphins are mammals.

pod (POD)—a small group of dolphins

Read More

Gowell, Elizabeth Tayntor. *Whales and Dolphins: What They Have in Common.* Animals In Order. New York: Franklin Watts, 2000.

Holmes, Kevin J. *Dolphins.* Animals. Mankato, Minn.: Bridgestone Books, 1998.

Internet Sites

All About Mammals
http://www.EnchantedLearning.com/subjects/mammals
Animals of the Sea
http://www.germantown.k12.il.us/html/animals1.html
Aqua Facts-Dolphins and Porpoises
http://oceanlink.island.net/aquafacts/dolphin.html

Index